Lights Of Love

An Advent And Christmas Eve Candlelight Service

By Charles T. Brown

C.S.S. Publishing Company, Inc.
Lima, Ohio

LIGHTS OF LOVE

9150 / ISBN 1-55673-351-8   PRINTED IN U.S.A.

TABLE OF CONTENTS

INTRODUCTION

There are many services for the lighting of the candles of the Advent wreath. This arrangement calls for the four — three violet and one pink — candles of the wreath, plus the fifth — white — candle in the center of the wreath.

It is suggested that different members of the congregation or Sunday school do the readings. The first candle is lighted on the first Sunday in Advent and the other three on succeeding Sundays. The fifth candle is lighted at the Christmas Eve candlelight service or on the service for Christmas day.

The actual candlelighting Scriptures, Messages and Prayers were developed by Rev. Charles T. Brown. The section titled "The Meaning Of Advent," is from **Lectionary Preaching Workbook, A** by John R. Brokhoff. The Call To Worships (optional material) are from **Lectionary Worship Aids C,** by Heth H. Corl. Both are published by C.S.S. Publishing Company.

THE MEANING OF ADVENT

Advent, a season of four Sundays, opens the church year. The season begins on the Sunday closest to St. Andrew's Day, November 30. The observance of Advent originated in France during the fourth century. The duration of the season varied from four to seven weeks until the Bishop of Rome in the sixth century set the season at four weeks. In ancient times Advent was strictly observed: every Christian was required to attend church services and fast daily.

The word, Advent, consists of two Latin word: **ad — venire,** "to come to." Advent's message is that God in Christ is coming to the world. This coming may be:

1. **A past experience.** God did come in Christ at Christmas. The prophets' promise was fulfilled in the Babe.
2. **A present experience.** God may come to you this Christmas in terms of rebirth, either for the first time, or a renewed birth in deeper dimensions of reality.
3. **A future experience.** Christ will return unpredictably at the end of the world. "He shall come again with glory to judge the quick and the dead."

The Message Of Advent

Since Advent promises the sure coming of the Lord, its message is "prepare." The Lord is coming whether the world is

5

ready or not. For those unprepared, his coming means judgment. For those ready for his coming, it means salvation.

How does Advent suggest that we prepare?

1. **Repentance** — forsake the sins of the world for a godly way of life.
2. **Prayer** — pray for the coming of Christ, for he shall save.
3. **Patience** — his coming may be delayed. Watch and wait, for his coming may be sudden.

The Mood Of Advent

1. **Expressed in color.** The mood of Advent is expressed in the liturgical color, violet. It depicts a feeling of quiet dignity, royalty, and repentance. Violet was the traditional color of a king's robe; the coming Christ is King of kings. Advent, like Lent, is a time for solemn and sober thought about one's sins, leading to repentance. It denotes a quiet time for watching, waiting, and praying for Christ to come again, either personally or universally. An alternate color for Advent is blue, the color of hope.

2. **Solemnity and sobriety.** Advent is a time to become aware of one's sins. Traditionally, Advent is a penitential season, originally known as the "Winter Lent." This mood of sobriety is expressed not only in the liturgical color, violet, but in the music of Advent hymns like "O Come, Emmanuel." During Advent choirs may omit processionals or have "silent processionals." Weddings in this season are discouraged. Christmas carols and decorations are often delayed until Christmas Eve.

3. **Joy in hope.** Advent stresses not so much fulfillment as anticipation of fulfillment: the Lord is coming! Christians have great expectations of Christ's coming again. As a family looks forward to a son returning from a war and as a bride anticipates her wedding day, so a Christian looks forward with joy to Christ's coming. Yet, this is a different kind of joy — a joy of hope amid solemnity. It is the quiet joy of

anticipation and not the joy of celebration of a past event. This type of joy is expressed in the Advent hymns: "Joy to the World, the Lord is come(ing), " and "O Come Emmanuel ... Rejoice, Rejoice, Emmanuel shall come to thee, O Israel."

The Observance Of Advent

Increasingly the church is beginning to observe Advent seriously as a vital and necessary time of preparation for a meaningful, spiritual Christmas. This observance is expressed in various ways:
1. Use of an Advent wreath in the church and homes.
2. Use of an Advent calendar for children in the home.
3. Discouragement of weddings and pre-Christmas parties.
4. Use of Advent hymns, prayers, and anthems throughout Advent.
5. Silent processionals during Advent.
6. Special mid-week Advent services.
7. Use of Advent symbols: Messianic rose, Tau cross, etc.
8. Preparation of Chrismons for decorating the Christmas tree.

FAITH

The First Advent Candle

"Now faith is the substance of things hoped for, the evidence of things not seen."
— Hebrews 11:1

Message:
The first candle of the Advent wreath is symbolic of faith. What great power true religious faith gives to a believer. The 11th chapter of the book of Hebrews gives such a noble record of steadfast people who lived so triumphantly by its sure light.

As we begin our Advent devotions we look to faith in God as a means to guide us to another celebration of the Nativity. We prepare the way of the Lord in the faith that many will come to follow his teachings, to know his truths and to accept his life. We have faith in the coming of his kingdom of God on earth as it is in heaven.

How we need this trust, this faith, to chase away skepticism and doubt and thus to allow our Christ-like lives to shine with hope amid the world's darkness and despair. It is because we have this faith in God's eternal triumph in the world, as manifested in his son Jesus Christ, we now light the candle of faith.

(Light the candle.)

8

Prayer:

Gracious God, as we make ready for the birth of Christ, prepare our hearts and minds to have faith in your eternal goodness and purpose for the world. In his name. Amen.

Optional Material:

Call To Worship

Pastor: Christian friends, we begin a new year in the church as we prepare for Christ's advent.

People: We thank God for this Advent season to remind us of the gift of his Son, and his promised return.

Pastor: Our thankfulness ought to result in an honest expression of love for one another, that we may be prepared for the advent of our Lord.

People: May God cause our love for one another to grow more and more.

Suggested Hymns For The First Sunday Of Advent

O Come, O Come, Emmanuel
Break Forth, O Living Light Of God
The King Shall Come
Joy To The World
Savior Of The Nations, Come
Fling Wide The Door, Unbar The Gate

HOPE

The Second Advent Candle

> *"For we are saved by hope: but hope that is seen is not hope: for what a man seeth, why doth he yet hope for?*
>
> *"But if we hope for that we see not, then do we with patience wait for it."*
> — Romans 8:24-25

Message:

The advent candle for the second Sunday is symbolic of hope. The first candle glows with a radiant faith in God, and from that religious light comes the sustaining quality of hope.

How well the prophet Isaiah has expressed a challenging hope for a better world. "Instead of the thorn shall come up the fir tree, and instead of the brier shall come up the myrtle tree: and it shall be to the Lord for a name, for an everlasting sign that shall not be cut off. (Isaiah 55:13)."

We have hope for the kingdom of God on earth. Christ has taught us to pray for this kingdom. As his followers we must believe in it and in the possibility of its fulfillment here on earth.

This Christian hope is the opposite of a dark and hopeless fatalism. The light of hope must shine upon our way today in

spite of atom bombs, terrorism and insecurity. This blessed
hope is possible because God sent his Son to reveal to all the
people of this earth the way to peace and goodwill.

So reverently we now light the candle of hope from the
shining candle of faith.

(Light the candle.)

Prayer:

O God we thank you for the hope that is in our hearts because Christ has revealed your love to us and has taught us
that you, our Father in heaven, have made of one blood all
people upon the earth. Amen.

Optional Material:
_____

Call To Worship

Pastor: The Lord is asking us to ready ourselves for his
coming

**People: We delight in the presence of our Lord. But we know
we are not fully prepared to receive him.**

Pastor: That is because we are guilty of sin. But God wants
to come and purify us, that we may be able to offer
our true worship

**People: Come to us, Lord, with cleansing, that we may please
you with our worship.**

Suggested Hymns For The Second Sunday Of Advent

Come, Thou Long-expected Jesus
God Of Our Life, Through All the Circling Years
Comfort, Comfort Now My People
On Jordan's Banks The Baptist's Cry
Prepare The Royal Highway
Hail To The Lord's Anointed
Let All Mortal Flesh Keep Silence

LOVE

The Third Advent Candle

"And now abideth faith, hope, love, these three: but the greatest of these is love."
— 1 Corinthians 13:13

Message:
The two previous candles of the Advent wreath have stood for faith and hope. The candle for this third Sunday symbolizes love.

Love has been used to describe God. Jesus as God's son gives us our greatest example of what love really is like. Our Lord is complete love.

Love is not used often enough in our everyday world. We often have scarcely tried it to see how well it can solve the many human problems in our day by day living.

How love graces the true home and God-centered family! There is the love of parents and the love of children and the whole family circle of loved ones. It is not easy perhaps to draw a specific picture of this love, but it is known by acts of kindness and feelings of mutual concern and affection.

How very much our whole world needs this kindness and this affection and this mutual trust and forbearance radiating from true love. It is needed not only at home and at church, in the classroom and in business and industry, but also in legislative halls and among the councils of nations.

May the light of love, as seen in the third Advent candle, burn brightly everywhere.

(Light the candles.)

Prayer:

O God of love, who showed us in your son the perfect expression of love, may this same love shine upon the ways and lives of all the people of the earth at Christmas and always. Amen.

Optional Material:
_____

Call To Worship

Pastor: God is constantly coming in our midst to renew us in love.

People: As we prepare for Christmas, we become more sensitive to the fact that we need God's love to be renewed in us.

Pastor: Then let us rejoice in the salvation to new life as God comes in our midst.

People: We come with gladness in our hearts to worship our God who comes with salvation!

Suggested Hymns For The Third Sunday Of Advent

Lift Up Your Heads, O Mighty Gates
O Day Of God, Draw Nigh
Of The Father's Love Begotten
As Pants The Hart
The Only Son From Heaven
Hark! A Thrilling Voice Is Sounding!
Hark, The Glad Sound! The Savior Comes

JOY

The Fourth Advent Candle

"And the angel said unto them, Fear not: for,
behold, I bring you good tidings of great joy,
which shall be to all people."

— Luke 2:10

Message:

The three candles in the Advent wreath now burning stand for faith, hope and love. These are all elements in a vital religious life and experience. We need these qualities of a firm religious belief for the day by day journey of life.

This season of the Christian year, however, brings us one more quality of heart and soul. It is that of joy. So the fourth candle symbolizes joy. "Joy to the world, the Lord is come," says one of our Christmas carols.

"And the shepherds returned, glorifying and praising God for all the things that they had heard and seen, as it was told unto them (Luke 2:20)."

Also the wisemen, "When they saw the star, they rejoiced with exceeding great joy (Matthew 2:10)."

We now light the candle for joy which burns so freely at Christmas because of Christ's birth. May joy burn brightly in the hearts of people everywhere.

(Light the candle.)

Prayer:
We thank you, O God, for the great joy that is ours because you have sent us the Christ Child. Help us to let our light of joy shine brightly that all may know of our faith, our hope, and our love. In Christ's name. Amen.

Optional Material:

Call To Worship
Pastor: Glad songs of Christ's birth fill the air with joy.
People: We sing in praise for God's gift of Christ, the Savior of the world!
Pastor: Christ is the perfect gift, offering complete atonement for sin, which brings us into a saving relationship with our God.
People: We have the assurance that Christ has come, and once for all has made atonement for our sins, and for the sins of the whole world.

Suggested Hymns For The Fourth Sunday Of Advent

Watchman, Tell Us Of The Night
Once In Royal David's City
Savior Of The Nations, Come
Lo, He comes With Clouds Descending
The King Shall Come
The People That In Darkness Sat
O Young And Fearless Prophet

THE LIGHT OF THE WORLD

The Christmas Candle

> *"Then spake Jesus again unto them, saying,
> I am the light of the world: he that followeth
> me shall not walk in darkness, but shall have
> the light of life."*
>
> — John 8:12

Message:

During the Advent season we have lighted four candles in the Advent wreath: one for faith, one for hope, one for love, and lastly, one for joy. As we come to the actual celebration of Christ's birth, we light a fifth candle. This candle sits in a different position in the wreath and is a different color, because no other candle can compare to it.

This fifth candle is symbolic of the light of the world, namely, Christ, our Lord. What good things this light brings to all of us, and how its radiance dispels the darkness of the earth. It gives us all the qualities of life represented in the other four candles of the Advent wreath.

There is always great expectation for the people of the earth because of this sacred Light, Jesus the Christ. On this Christmas may this Light shine brightly to cast out the darkness of sorrow, wrong, and hatred in the lives of people. Indeed, at this holy season may Christ's light — like faith, hope, love, and joy, glow in the hearts and lives of people everywhere.

(Light the candle.)

Prayer:
Brighten, O God, all the world this Christmas with the light of the world, even thy Son, Jesus, our Lord and Savior. Amen.

Optional Material:

Call To Worship
Pastor: Joy has come to our world! The Savior is born!
People: All heaven and earth sing for joy. God has come to the people!
Pastor: Let every heart be receptive to God's gift of salvation in Jesus, his son.
People: May the Son of God, born in Bethlehem, be born in us today.

Suggested Hymns For Use On Christmas Eve

Away In The Manger
Angels From The Realms Of Glory
Angels We Have Heard On High
Gentle Mary Laid Her Child
Hark! The Herald Angels Sing
In The Bleak Midwinter
Joy To The World
Silent Night, Holy Night
What Child Is This
While Shepherds Watched Their Flocks

SERVICE FOR CHRISTMAS EVE

Scripture — Hebrews 1:11
Lighting the first candle
Message
Prayer
Hymn — "Come, O Come, Emmanuel" (v. 1)

Scripture — Romans 8:24-25
Lighting the second candle
Message
Prayer
Hymn — "Come, Thou Long-expected Jesus" (v. 1)

Scripture — 1 Corinthians 13:13
Lighting the third candle
Message
Prayer
Hymn — "Lift Up Your Heads, O Mighty Gates" (v. 1)

Scripture — Luke 2:10
Lighting the fourth candle
Message
Prayer
Hymn — "Watchman, Tell Us Of The Night" (v. 1)

Scripture — John 8:12
Lighting the Christmas candle
Message
Prayer
Hymn — "Away In The Manger" (v. 1)

Benediction

THE BANNER

As a worship enhancement to your Advent celebration you might ask someone in your congregation to create an Advent banner. The suggested banner in this booklet follows the theme of "Lights Of Love."

Suggested dimensions of the banner are four by six feet (on the grid, one inch equals one foot). Suggested colors are lavender or white. The colors of the candles are, from left: purple or violet for Advent 1, purple or violet for Advent 2, white for the large center candle of Christmas Eve, pink for Advent 3, and purple or violet for Advent 4.

If you use a different color pattern for your Advent wreath you should substitute the appropriate colors in your banner.

As an additional thought, you might develop your banner with Velcro on the back of each candle. As you light each week's Advent wreath candle you could have a child in your congregation place the appropriate candle on the banner. This could extend to Christmas Eve, where you might remove all the candles and place each one again on the banner at the appropriate time in the service.

Turn the page for the banner grid.

Scale 1 inch (square) = 1 foot

20

www.ingramcontent.com/pod-product-compliance
Lightning Source LLC
Chambersburg PA
CBHW060045040426
42331CB00032B/2480